50 Classic American Dishes Recipes

By: Kelly Johnson

Table of Contents

- Apple Pie
- Beef Stew
- Buffalo Wings
- Meatloaf
- Fried Chicken
- Clam Chowder
- Grilled Cheese Sandwich
- Macaroni and Cheese
- Pulled Pork Sandwiches
- Chicago Deep-Dish Pizza
- New England Lobster Roll
- Philly Cheesesteak
- Biscuits and Gravy
- BBQ Ribs
- Hot Dogs
- Chicken Pot Pie
- BLT Sandwich
- Cobb Salad
- Sloppy Joes
- Pancakes with Maple Syrup
- Cornbread
- Tuna Casserole
- Shrimp and Grits
- Caesar Salad
- Pot Roast
- Caesar Salad
- Chopped Cheese Sandwich
- Baked Ziti
- Shepherd's Pie
- Chili Con Carne
- Hush Puppies
- Roast Turkey with Stuffing
- Caesar Salad with Grilled Chicken
- Lobster Bisque
- Chicken Fried Steak

- Beef Tacos
- Stuffed Bell Peppers
- Egg Salad Sandwiches
- Jambalaya
- Philly Pretzels
- Fettuccine Alfredo
- Cobbler (Peach or Berry)
- Grilled Salmon with Dill Sauce
- Fish Tacos
- French Dip Sandwich
- Shrimp Cocktail
- Cheese and Onion Quesadillas
- Southern Grits
- Stuffed Mushrooms
- Bagel with Lox and Cream Cheese

Apple Pie
Ingredients:

- 6-7 medium apples (Granny Smith or Honeycrisp), peeled and sliced
- 1 cup granulated sugar
- 1 tablespoon lemon juice
- 1 teaspoon ground cinnamon
- 1 tablespoon all-purpose flour
- 1/2 teaspoon ground nutmeg
- 1 tablespoon unsalted butter
- 1 package refrigerated pie crusts

Instructions:

1. Preheat oven to 425°F (220°C).
2. In a large bowl, toss apples with sugar, lemon juice, cinnamon, nutmeg, and flour.
3. Roll out one pie crust and fit it into a pie pan.
4. Fill the crust with the apple mixture and dot with butter.
5. Cover with the second pie crust and trim any excess dough.
6. Bake for 45-50 minutes or until crust is golden brown and apples are tender.

Beef Stew
Ingredients:

- 1 lb beef chuck, cut into cubes
- 4 cups beef broth
- 2 carrots, peeled and sliced
- 3 potatoes, peeled and diced
- 1 onion, chopped
- 2 cloves garlic, minced
- 1/2 cup red wine (optional)
- 1 teaspoon dried thyme
- 2 bay leaves
- Salt and pepper to taste
- 2 tablespoons olive oil

Instructions:

1. Heat olive oil in a large pot over medium heat. Brown the beef cubes on all sides, then remove and set aside.
2. In the same pot, sauté onion and garlic until softened.
3. Return beef to the pot and add broth, red wine (if using), thyme, bay leaves, carrots, and potatoes.
4. Bring to a simmer, then cover and cook for 1.5-2 hours, or until beef is tender.
5. Season with salt and pepper and serve hot.

Buffalo Wings
Ingredients:

- 2 lbs chicken wings
- 1/2 cup hot sauce
- 1/4 cup unsalted butter, melted
- 1 tablespoon white vinegar
- 1/4 teaspoon garlic powder
- Salt and pepper to taste

Instructions:

1. Preheat oven to 400°F (200°C).
2. Season wings with salt and pepper and place on a baking sheet.
3. Bake for 40-45 minutes, flipping halfway through, until crispy.
4. In a bowl, mix hot sauce, melted butter, vinegar, and garlic powder.
5. Toss cooked wings in the sauce and serve immediately.

Meatloaf
Ingredients:

- 1 lb ground beef
- 1/2 lb ground pork
- 1 onion, chopped
- 1 cup breadcrumbs
- 1/2 cup milk
- 1 egg
- 1/4 cup ketchup
- 1 tablespoon Worcestershire sauce
- Salt and pepper to taste

Instructions:

1. Preheat oven to 350°F (175°C).
2. In a large bowl, combine all ingredients. Mix until well combined.
3. Shape the mixture into a loaf and place on a baking sheet.
4. Bake for 45-50 minutes or until the meatloaf is cooked through.
5. Let rest for 10 minutes before slicing and serving.

Fried Chicken
Ingredients:

- 4 chicken thighs, bone-in, skin-on
- 1 cup buttermilk
- 1 cup all-purpose flour
- 1 teaspoon paprika
- 1 teaspoon garlic powder
- Salt and pepper to taste
- Vegetable oil for frying

Instructions:

1. Marinate chicken in buttermilk for at least 2 hours, or overnight.
2. In a bowl, mix flour, paprika, garlic powder, salt, and pepper.
3. Heat oil in a deep skillet to 350°F (175°C).
4. Coat chicken in the flour mixture, shaking off excess.
5. Fry chicken for 10-12 minutes, turning halfway, until golden brown and cooked through.
6. Drain on paper towels and serve.

Clam Chowder
Ingredients:

- 2 cans (6.5 oz each) chopped clams, drained, juice reserved
- 1 cup diced potatoes
- 1/2 cup celery, chopped
- 1/2 cup onion, chopped
- 2 cups heavy cream
- 2 tablespoons butter
- 1/2 teaspoon thyme
- Salt and pepper to taste

Instructions:

1. In a large pot, melt butter and sauté onions and celery until soft.
2. Add potatoes, clam juice, and thyme. Simmer until potatoes are tender (about 10-15 minutes).
3. Add clams and heavy cream. Stir and heat until warm.
4. Season with salt and pepper, then serve.

Grilled Cheese Sandwich

Ingredients:

- 2 slices bread
- 2 slices cheese (cheddar, American, or your choice)
- 1 tablespoon butter

Instructions:

1. Butter one side of each slice of bread.
2. Place cheese between the unbuttered sides of the bread.
3. Heat a skillet over medium heat. Place the sandwich in the skillet and cook until golden brown, 2-3 minutes per side.
4. Serve hot.

Macaroni and Cheese
Ingredients:

- 8 oz elbow macaroni
- 2 cups shredded cheddar cheese
- 1 cup milk
- 2 tablespoons butter
- 2 tablespoons all-purpose flour
- Salt and pepper to taste

Instructions:

1. Cook macaroni according to package instructions and drain.
2. In a saucepan, melt butter and whisk in flour to create a roux.
3. Gradually add milk, whisking constantly until the sauce thickens.
4. Stir in cheese until melted and smooth.
5. Combine with cooked macaroni and serve.

Pulled Pork Sandwiches
Ingredients:

- 2 lbs pork shoulder
- 1 cup BBQ sauce
- 1/2 cup apple cider vinegar
- 1 tablespoon brown sugar
- 1 teaspoon smoked paprika
- Salt and pepper to taste
- 6 sandwich buns

Instructions:

1. Preheat oven to 325°F (165°C).
2. Season pork shoulder with paprika, salt, and pepper.
3. Place in a roasting pan with BBQ sauce, vinegar, and brown sugar.
4. Cover and cook for 3-4 hours, until tender.
5. Shred pork with a fork and serve on buns with additional BBQ sauce.

Chicago Deep-Dish Pizza
Ingredients:

- 1 1/2 cups all-purpose flour
- 1/4 cup cornmeal
- 1 teaspoon salt
- 1/2 teaspoon sugar
- 1/4 ounce active dry yeast
- 1 cup warm water
- 1/4 cup olive oil
- 2 cups mozzarella cheese, shredded
- 1 cup Parmesan cheese, grated
- 1 can (28 oz) crushed tomatoes
- 1 tablespoon tomato paste
- 1 teaspoon dried oregano
- 1 teaspoon dried basil
- 1/2 teaspoon garlic powder
- 1/4 lb Italian sausage, crumbled
- 1/2 onion, chopped
- 1 bell pepper, chopped

Instructions:

1. Preheat oven to 475°F (245°C).
2. Mix flour, cornmeal, salt, sugar, and yeast in a bowl. Add warm water and olive oil, then knead the dough for about 5 minutes until smooth. Let it rise for 1 hour.
3. Cook sausage, onion, and bell pepper in a pan until browned. Add crushed tomatoes, tomato paste, oregano, basil, and garlic powder, then simmer for 10 minutes.
4. Roll dough into a round shape and press into a deep-dish pizza pan.
5. Layer cheese, sausage mixture, and the remaining mozzarella and Parmesan cheeses.
6. Bake for 30-40 minutes, or until the crust is golden and the cheese is bubbly.

New England Lobster Roll
Ingredients:

- 1 lb lobster meat, cooked and chopped
- 1/4 cup mayonnaise
- 1 tablespoon lemon juice
- 1 tablespoon fresh parsley, chopped
- Salt and pepper to taste
- 4 hot dog buns, toasted
- 2 tablespoons butter

Instructions:

1. Mix the lobster meat, mayonnaise, lemon juice, parsley, salt, and pepper in a bowl.
2. Melt butter in a skillet and toast the buns until golden brown.
3. Fill each bun with the lobster mixture and serve immediately.

Philly Cheesesteak
Ingredients:

- 1 lb ribeye steak, thinly sliced
- 1 tablespoon olive oil
- 1 onion, sliced
- 1 bell pepper, sliced
- 4 hoagie rolls
- 8 slices provolone cheese
- Salt and pepper to taste

Instructions:

1. Heat olive oil in a pan and cook onion and bell pepper until softened.
2. Season the steak with salt and pepper, then cook in the same pan until browned.
3. Place the provolone cheese over the steak and melt.
4. Split the rolls and fill them with the steak and vegetable mixture. Serve hot.

Biscuits and Gravy
Ingredients:

- 1 can refrigerated biscuit dough
- 1 lb breakfast sausage
- 1/4 cup all-purpose flour
- 2 cups milk
- Salt and pepper to taste

Instructions:

1. Preheat oven and bake the biscuits according to the package directions.
2. Cook sausage in a skillet, breaking it apart as it cooks.
3. Stir in flour and cook for 1-2 minutes.
4. Slowly add milk and stir until the gravy thickens.
5. Season with salt and pepper, then pour the gravy over the biscuits.

BBQ Ribs
Ingredients:

- 2 racks of baby back ribs
- 1/4 cup brown sugar
- 1 tablespoon smoked paprika
- 1 tablespoon garlic powder
- 1 tablespoon onion powder
- 1 teaspoon chili powder
- Salt and pepper to taste
- 1 cup BBQ sauce

Instructions:

1. Preheat oven to 300°F (150°C).
2. Mix the dry ingredients to make the rub.
3. Rub the ribs with the seasoning mix and place on a baking sheet.
4. Cover with foil and bake for 2.5 hours.
5. Brush ribs with BBQ sauce and bake for an additional 30 minutes.

Hot Dogs
Ingredients:

- 4 hot dog buns
- 4 beef hot dogs
- Mustard, ketchup, relish, onions, or any toppings of your choice

Instructions:

1. Grill or boil the hot dogs until heated through.
2. Place the hot dogs in the buns and add your favorite toppings.

Chicken Pot Pie
Ingredients:

- 2 cups cooked chicken, shredded
- 1 cup frozen mixed vegetables
- 1 can (10.5 oz) cream of chicken soup
- 1/2 cup milk
- 1 package refrigerated pie crusts
- Salt and pepper to taste

Instructions:

1. Preheat oven to 400°F (200°C).
2. In a bowl, mix chicken, vegetables, soup, milk, salt, and pepper.
3. Place one pie crust in a pie pan and add the chicken mixture.
4. Top with the second pie crust and crimp the edges.
5. Bake for 30-35 minutes until golden brown.

BLT Sandwich

Ingredients:

- 4 slices of bacon
- 2 slices of bread, toasted
- 2 leaves of lettuce
- 2 slices of tomato
- Mayonnaise

Instructions:

1. Cook the bacon until crispy.
2. Spread mayonnaise on both slices of toasted bread.
3. Layer bacon, lettuce, and tomato on one slice of bread.
4. Top with the second slice of bread and serve.

Cobb Salad
Ingredients:

- 2 cups mixed greens
- 1/2 cup cooked chicken breast, chopped
- 1/2 avocado, sliced
- 2 hard-boiled eggs, chopped
- 1/4 cup blue cheese, crumbled
- 1/4 cup bacon bits
- 1/2 cup tomato, chopped
- 1/4 cup ranch dressing

Instructions:

1. Arrange greens on a plate.
2. Arrange the remaining ingredients in rows on top of the greens.
3. Drizzle with ranch dressing and serve.

Sloppy Joes
Ingredients:

- 1 lb ground beef
- 1 small onion, chopped
- 1/2 cup ketchup
- 1 tablespoon mustard
- 1 tablespoon brown sugar
- 1 teaspoon Worcestershire sauce
- 4 sandwich buns

Instructions:

1. Cook ground beef and onion in a pan until browned.
2. Add ketchup, mustard, brown sugar, and Worcestershire sauce.
3. Simmer for 10-15 minutes.
4. Spoon the mixture onto the sandwich buns and serve.

Pancakes with Maple Syrup
Ingredients:

- 1 cup all-purpose flour
- 1 tablespoon sugar
- 1 tablespoon baking powder
- 1/2 teaspoon salt
- 1 egg
- 1 cup milk
- 2 tablespoons melted butter
- Maple syrup

Instructions:

1. Mix dry ingredients in a bowl.
2. In another bowl, whisk egg, milk, and melted butter.
3. Combine wet and dry ingredients until smooth.
4. Heat a skillet over medium heat and cook pancakes until golden brown.
5. Serve with maple syrup.

Cornbread
Ingredients:

- 1 cup cornmeal
- 1 cup all-purpose flour
- 1/4 cup sugar
- 1 tablespoon baking powder
- 1/2 teaspoon salt
- 1 cup milk
- 2 eggs
- 1/4 cup unsalted butter, melted

Instructions:

1. Preheat oven to 400°F (200°C).
2. Mix dry ingredients in a bowl.
3. In another bowl, whisk milk, eggs, and melted butter.
4. Combine wet and dry ingredients until just mixed.
5. Pour batter into a greased pan and bake for 20-25 minutes until golden brown.

Tuna Casserole
Ingredients:

- 2 cans (5 oz each) tuna in oil, drained
- 1 cup cooked pasta (e.g., elbow macaroni)
- 1 can (10.5 oz) cream of mushroom soup
- 1/2 cup milk
- 1/2 cup frozen peas
- 1/2 cup shredded cheddar cheese
- 1/4 cup breadcrumbs
- 2 tablespoons butter, melted
- Salt and pepper to taste

Instructions:

1. Preheat oven to 350°F (175°C).
2. In a mixing bowl, combine tuna, pasta, soup, milk, peas, and cheese. Season with salt and pepper.
3. Pour the mixture into a greased casserole dish.
4. In a small bowl, combine breadcrumbs and melted butter, then sprinkle over the casserole.
5. Bake for 25-30 minutes, until golden and bubbly.

Shrimp and Grits
Ingredients:

- 1 lb shrimp, peeled and deveined
- 1 cup grits
- 4 cups water or chicken broth
- 1/2 cup heavy cream
- 1/4 cup butter
- 1 teaspoon garlic, minced
- 1 tablespoon lemon juice
- 1 tablespoon parsley, chopped
- Salt and pepper to taste

Instructions:

1. Bring water or chicken broth to a boil, then stir in grits. Reduce heat and cook according to package instructions.
2. In a skillet, melt butter and sauté garlic until fragrant. Add shrimp, salt, pepper, and lemon juice, cooking for 3-4 minutes until pink.
3. Stir heavy cream into grits and cook for 2 more minutes.
4. Serve shrimp over the creamy grits, garnished with parsley.

Caesar Salad
Ingredients:

- 4 cups Romaine lettuce, chopped
- 1/4 cup Caesar dressing
- 1/4 cup Parmesan cheese, grated
- Croutons

Instructions:

1. Toss chopped lettuce with Caesar dressing.
2. Add grated Parmesan and croutons on top.
3. Serve immediately.

Pot Roast
Ingredients:

- 3 lb beef chuck roast
- 1 onion, chopped
- 4 carrots, chopped
- 4 potatoes, chopped
- 2 cups beef broth
- 1 tablespoon Worcestershire sauce
- 1 teaspoon thyme
- Salt and pepper to taste

Instructions:

1. Preheat oven to 325°F (160°C).
2. Sear the roast in a hot pan with oil on all sides.
3. Place roast in a large pot with onions, carrots, potatoes, beef broth, Worcestershire sauce, thyme, salt, and pepper.
4. Cover and bake for 3-4 hours, until tender.
5. Serve the roast with vegetables.

Caesar Salad
Ingredients:

- 4 cups romaine lettuce, chopped
- 1/2 cup Caesar dressing
- 1/2 cup grated Parmesan cheese
- 1 cup croutons
- 1 teaspoon anchovy paste (optional)
- Freshly ground black pepper to taste

Instructions:

1. In a large bowl, toss the chopped romaine lettuce with the Caesar dressing until evenly coated.
2. Add grated Parmesan cheese and toss again.
3. Top with croutons and optional anchovy paste for added flavor.
4. Season with freshly ground black pepper to taste.
5. Serve immediately as a fresh and satisfying side dish or light meal.

Chopped Cheese Sandwich
Ingredients:

- 1 lb ground beef
- 1 onion, chopped
- 4 sandwich rolls
- 4 slices American cheese
- Ketchup, mustard, or any condiments you like
- Salt and pepper to taste

Instructions:

1. Cook ground beef in a skillet, breaking it up as it cooks. Add onions and cook until softened.
2. Season with salt and pepper.
3. Toast sandwich rolls and assemble with the beef mixture and a slice of cheese on top.
4. Add your preferred condiments and serve.

Baked Ziti
Ingredients:

- 1 lb ziti pasta, cooked
- 2 cups marinara sauce
- 1 cup ricotta cheese
- 2 cups mozzarella cheese, shredded
- 1/2 cup Parmesan cheese, grated
- 1 teaspoon dried oregano
- Salt and pepper to taste

Instructions:

1. Preheat oven to 375°F (190°C).
2. In a large bowl, combine cooked pasta with marinara sauce, ricotta, 1 cup mozzarella, Parmesan, oregano, salt, and pepper.
3. Transfer mixture into a greased baking dish.
4. Sprinkle remaining mozzarella on top and bake for 25-30 minutes.
5. Serve hot.

Shepherd's Pie
Ingredients:

- 1 lb ground lamb or beef
- 1 onion, chopped
- 1 cup frozen peas
- 2 cups mashed potatoes
- 1 cup beef broth
- 1 tablespoon tomato paste
- 1 teaspoon thyme
- Salt and pepper to taste

Instructions:

1. Preheat oven to 400°F (200°C).
2. Brown the ground meat with onions in a pan, then stir in peas, broth, tomato paste, thyme, salt, and pepper.
3. Transfer meat mixture into a baking dish, then spread mashed potatoes on top.
4. Bake for 20 minutes, until golden brown.

Chili Con Carne

Ingredients:

- 1 lb ground beef
- 1 onion, chopped
- 1 can (15 oz) kidney beans, drained
- 1 can (15 oz) diced tomatoes
- 1 tablespoon chili powder
- 1 teaspoon cumin
- Salt and pepper to taste

Instructions:

1. Brown the ground beef with onions in a large pot.
2. Stir in beans, tomatoes, chili powder, cumin, salt, and pepper.
3. Simmer for 30-40 minutes.
4. Serve hot, optionally with toppings like cheese or sour cream.

Hush Puppies
Ingredients:

- 1 cup cornmeal
- 1/2 cup flour
- 1 teaspoon baking powder
- 1/4 teaspoon salt
- 1/2 teaspoon sugar
- 1/4 cup milk
- 1 egg
- 1/4 cup onion, chopped
- Vegetable oil for frying

Instructions:

1. In a bowl, combine cornmeal, flour, baking powder, salt, and sugar.
2. Stir in milk, egg, and onions.
3. Heat oil in a pan and drop spoonfuls of batter into the oil.
4. Fry until golden brown, then drain on paper towels.

Roast Turkey with Stuffing
Ingredients:

- 1 whole turkey (10-12 lbs)
- 2 tablespoons olive oil
- 2 teaspoons salt
- 1 teaspoon pepper
- 2 cups bread cubes
- 1/2 cup butter
- 1 onion, chopped
- 2 cups chicken broth
- 1 teaspoon sage

Instructions:

1. Preheat oven to 325°F (160°C).
2. Rub turkey with olive oil, salt, and pepper.
3. Stuff turkey with prepared stuffing made by cooking onions in butter, then adding bread cubes, chicken broth, and sage.
4. Roast turkey for 3-4 hours, or until internal temperature reaches 165°F (74°C).

Caesar Salad with Grilled Chicken

Ingredients:

- 4 cups Romaine lettuce, chopped
- 2 grilled chicken breasts, sliced
- 1/4 cup Caesar dressing
- 1/4 cup Parmesan cheese, grated
- Croutons

Instructions:

1. Toss lettuce with Caesar dressing.
2. Add grilled chicken, Parmesan, and croutons on top.
3. Serve immediately.

Lobster Bisque

Ingredients:

- 2 lobster tails, cooked and chopped
- 1/4 cup butter
- 1 onion, chopped
- 2 cloves garlic, minced
- 1/4 cup flour
- 4 cups seafood or chicken broth
- 1 cup heavy cream
- Salt and pepper to taste

Instructions:

1. In a pot, melt butter and sauté onion and garlic until soft.
2. Stir in flour and cook for 2 minutes.
3. Slowly add broth, stirring constantly, then bring to a simmer for 10 minutes.
4. Stir in cream and lobster, cooking until heated through.
5. Serve hot.

Chicken Fried Steak
Ingredients:

- 4 beef cube steaks
- 1 cup all-purpose flour
- 1 teaspoon garlic powder
- 1 teaspoon onion powder
- 1 teaspoon paprika
- Salt and pepper to taste
- 2 eggs, beaten
- 1/2 cup buttermilk
- Vegetable oil for frying

Instructions:

1. In a shallow bowl, combine flour, garlic powder, onion powder, paprika, salt, and pepper.
2. In another bowl, whisk together eggs and buttermilk.
3. Dredge each steak in the flour mixture, then dip it into the egg mixture, and coat again with flour.
4. Heat oil in a skillet over medium heat and fry the steaks for 3-4 minutes per side, until golden brown and cooked through.
5. Serve hot with gravy (optional).

Beef Tacos
Ingredients:

- 1 lb ground beef
- 1 onion, chopped
- 1 packet taco seasoning
- 1/2 cup water
- Taco shells
- Toppings: shredded lettuce, diced tomatoes, shredded cheese, sour cream, salsa

Instructions:

1. In a skillet, cook ground beef and onions over medium heat until browned.
2. Add taco seasoning and water, simmer for 5-7 minutes.
3. Spoon the beef mixture into taco shells and add your favorite toppings.
4. Serve immediately.

Stuffed Bell Peppers
Ingredients:

- 4 bell peppers, tops cut off and seeds removed
- 1 lb ground beef or turkey
- 1 cup cooked rice
- 1 can (15 oz) diced tomatoes
- 1 teaspoon Italian seasoning
- Salt and pepper to taste
- 1 cup shredded cheese (optional)

Instructions:

1. Preheat oven to 375°F (190°C).
2. In a skillet, cook ground beef (or turkey) until browned. Add cooked rice, diced tomatoes, Italian seasoning, salt, and pepper.
3. Stuff the peppers with the meat and rice mixture, then place in a baking dish.
4. Cover with foil and bake for 30 minutes.
5. Top with shredded cheese (optional) and bake for another 10 minutes.

Egg Salad Sandwiches
Ingredients:

- 6 hard-boiled eggs, chopped
- 1/4 cup mayonnaise
- 1 tablespoon mustard
- Salt and pepper to taste
- Bread slices
- Lettuce (optional)

Instructions:

1. In a bowl, mix chopped eggs, mayonnaise, mustard, salt, and pepper until well combined.
2. Spread egg salad on slices of bread.
3. Add lettuce (optional) and serve immediately.

Jambalaya
Ingredients:

- 1 lb chicken breast, diced
- 1 lb sausage, sliced
- 1 bell pepper, chopped
- 1 onion, chopped
- 2 cloves garlic, minced
- 1 can (14.5 oz) diced tomatoes
- 2 cups chicken broth
- 1 1/2 cups long-grain rice
- 1 tablespoon Cajun seasoning
- Salt and pepper to taste

Instructions:

1. In a large pot, cook chicken and sausage over medium heat until browned.
2. Add bell pepper, onion, and garlic, cooking until softened.
3. Stir in diced tomatoes, chicken broth, rice, Cajun seasoning, salt, and pepper.
4. Bring to a simmer, cover, and cook for 20-25 minutes, until rice is tender.
5. Serve hot.

Philly Pretzels
Ingredients:

- 1 packet active dry yeast
- 1 cup warm water
- 1 tablespoon sugar
- 4 cups all-purpose flour
- 1 teaspoon salt
- 2 tablespoons melted butter
- Baking soda (for boiling)
- Coarse salt for sprinkling

Instructions:

1. In a bowl, dissolve yeast and sugar in warm water. Let sit for 5 minutes to activate.
2. Add flour, salt, and melted butter to the yeast mixture, and knead until smooth.
3. Let dough rise for 1 hour, then punch it down and divide into 8 pieces.
4. Roll each piece into a rope and shape into a pretzel.
5. Boil pretzels in water with baking soda for 30 seconds, then place on a baking sheet.
6. Sprinkle with coarse salt and bake at 400°F (200°C) for 12-15 minutes, until golden brown.

Fettuccine Alfredo
Ingredients:

- 1 lb fettuccine pasta
- 1/2 cup butter
- 1 cup heavy cream
- 1 1/2 cups grated Parmesan cheese
- 2 cloves garlic, minced
- Salt and pepper to taste
- Fresh parsley, chopped (optional)

Instructions:

1. Cook fettuccine according to package instructions. Drain and set aside.
2. In a pan, melt butter over medium heat and sauté garlic until fragrant.
3. Add heavy cream and bring to a simmer. Cook for 3-4 minutes until thickened.
4. Stir in Parmesan cheese, salt, and pepper until smooth.
5. Toss cooked fettuccine in the sauce, then serve garnished with parsley.

Cobbler (Peach or Berry)
Ingredients:

- 4 cups fruit (peach slices or mixed berries)
- 1/2 cup sugar
- 1 tablespoon cornstarch
- 1 teaspoon lemon juice
- 1 cup all-purpose flour
- 1/2 cup sugar
- 1 teaspoon baking powder
- 1/4 teaspoon salt
- 1/2 cup milk
- 1/4 cup butter, melted

Instructions:

1. Preheat oven to 375°F (190°C).
2. In a bowl, combine fruit, sugar, cornstarch, and lemon juice. Pour into a greased baking dish.
3. In another bowl, combine flour, sugar, baking powder, and salt. Stir in milk and melted butter to form a batter.
4. Spoon batter over the fruit mixture.
5. Bake for 30-40 minutes, until golden brown and bubbly.
6. Serve warm with vanilla ice cream or whipped cream.

Grilled Salmon with Dill Sauce

Ingredients:

- 4 salmon fillets
- 2 tablespoons olive oil
- Salt and pepper to taste
- 1/2 cup sour cream
- 2 tablespoons mayonnaise
- 1 tablespoon fresh dill, chopped
- 1 teaspoon lemon juice

Instructions:

1. Preheat the grill to medium heat.
2. Brush salmon fillets with olive oil and season with salt and pepper.
3. Grill the salmon for 4-5 minutes per side, until cooked through and flaky.
4. In a small bowl, mix together sour cream, mayonnaise, dill, and lemon juice.
5. Serve the grilled salmon with the dill sauce on the side.

Fish Tacos
Ingredients:

- 1 lb white fish (such as cod or tilapia), cut into strips
- 1 teaspoon chili powder
- 1 teaspoon cumin
- 1/2 teaspoon paprika
- Salt and pepper to taste
- 8 small corn tortillas
- Toppings: shredded cabbage, salsa, avocado, lime wedges, cilantro

Instructions:

1. In a bowl, mix chili powder, cumin, paprika, salt, and pepper. Toss the fish strips in the seasoning.
2. Heat a skillet over medium heat and cook the fish for 2-3 minutes per side, until cooked through.
3. Warm the tortillas and assemble the tacos by placing the fish in each tortilla.
4. Top with shredded cabbage, salsa, avocado, lime wedges, and cilantro. Serve immediately.

French Dip Sandwich
Ingredients:

- 1 lb roast beef, thinly sliced
- 4 hoagie rolls
- 2 cups beef broth
- 1 tablespoon soy sauce
- 1/2 teaspoon garlic powder
- 1/4 teaspoon black pepper
- 2 tablespoons butter
- 1/2 onion, sliced (optional)

Instructions:

1. In a saucepan, heat the beef broth, soy sauce, garlic powder, and pepper over medium heat, simmering for 5 minutes.
2. Split the hoagie rolls and butter each half.
3. Pile thin slices of roast beef onto the rolls and top with optional sautéed onions.
4. Serve with the warm beef broth for dipping.

Shrimp Cocktail
Ingredients:

- 1 lb large shrimp, peeled and deveined
- 1 tablespoon lemon juice
- 1 tablespoon Old Bay seasoning
- Cocktail sauce: 1/2 cup ketchup, 1 tablespoon horseradish, 1 tablespoon lemon juice, a dash of hot sauce

Instructions:

1. Bring a pot of water to a boil and add lemon juice and Old Bay seasoning.
2. Add shrimp and cook for 2-3 minutes, until pink and opaque.
3. Remove shrimp and cool in an ice bath.
4. Mix cocktail sauce ingredients and serve with shrimp chilled.

Cheese and Onion Quesadillas
Ingredients:

- 4 flour tortillas
- 1 cup shredded cheddar cheese
- 1/2 cup shredded Monterey Jack cheese
- 1 onion, thinly sliced
- 1 tablespoon olive oil
- Sour cream and salsa for serving

Instructions:

1. Heat olive oil in a skillet over medium heat and sauté onions until soft.
2. Lay a tortilla in a separate skillet and sprinkle with a mixture of both cheeses.
3. Add sautéed onions, top with another tortilla, and cook for 2-3 minutes per side, until golden and melted.
4. Slice into wedges and serve with sour cream and salsa.

Southern Grits

Ingredients:

- 1 cup stone-ground grits
- 4 cups water
- 1 tablespoon butter
- 1/2 cup milk
- Salt and pepper to taste
- 1/4 cup grated cheese (optional)

Instructions:

1. Bring water to a boil in a pot, then add grits and a pinch of salt.
2. Reduce heat to low, stirring occasionally. Cook for 20-25 minutes, until thickened.
3. Stir in butter, milk, and cheese (optional) for a creamy texture.
4. Season with salt and pepper and serve hot.

Stuffed Mushrooms
Ingredients:

- 12 large mushroom caps, cleaned and stems removed
- 1/2 cup cream cheese, softened
- 1/4 cup grated Parmesan cheese
- 1/4 cup breadcrumbs
- 1 tablespoon fresh parsley, chopped
- 1 tablespoon olive oil
- Salt and pepper to taste

Instructions:

1. Preheat oven to 375°F (190°C).
2. In a bowl, mix cream cheese, Parmesan cheese, breadcrumbs, parsley, salt, and pepper.
3. Stuff the mushroom caps with the mixture and place them on a baking sheet.
4. Drizzle with olive oil and bake for 20-25 minutes, until golden.

Bagel with Lox and Cream Cheese
Ingredients:

- 4 bagels, halved and toasted
- 4 ounces cream cheese
- 4 ounces smoked salmon (lox)
- 1/2 red onion, thinly sliced
- Capers (optional)
- Fresh dill (optional)

Instructions:

1. Spread cream cheese on the toasted bagel halves.
2. Top with smoked salmon, red onion, capers, and fresh dill.
3. Serve immediately as a delicious breakfast or brunch option.

www.ingramcontent.com/pod-product-compliance
Lightning Source LLC
LaVergne TN
LVHW081333060526
838201LV00055B/2617